For Milly, Oscar and all little explorers - M.B.

For Eva, Iván and Olov - J.V.

First published 2020
by Nosy Crow Ltd
The Crow's Nest, 14 Baden Place
Crosby Row, London SE1 1YW
www.nosycrow.com

ISBN 978 1 78800 406 0 (HB)
ISBN 978 1 78800 501 2 (PB)

A CIP catalogue record for this book is available from the British Library.

Printed in China

Papers used by Nosy Crow are made from wood grown in sustainable forests.

10 9 8 7 6 5 4 3 2 1 (HB)
10 9 8 7 6 5 4 3 2 1 (PB)

MOIRA BUTTERFIELD

JESÚS VERONA

LOOK WHAT I FOUND

in the Woods

nosy crow

Follow me. I know the way.
We're walking through the woods today.

Look what I found!

A curly stick to wave like a magic wand.

WOODS

Can you also see . . . ?

One signpost to show the way

Two butterflies fluttering

Three bright yellow flowers

A tree's branches and leaves are called its crown. Crowns grow in different shapes and sizes.

Some are tall and pointed . . .

and some spread out widely.

Sometimes trees have other plants growing on them. Look out for powdery green or orange algae (*al-gee*), grey splodges of lichen or cushions of furry green moss.

TREE SHAPES TO SPOT:

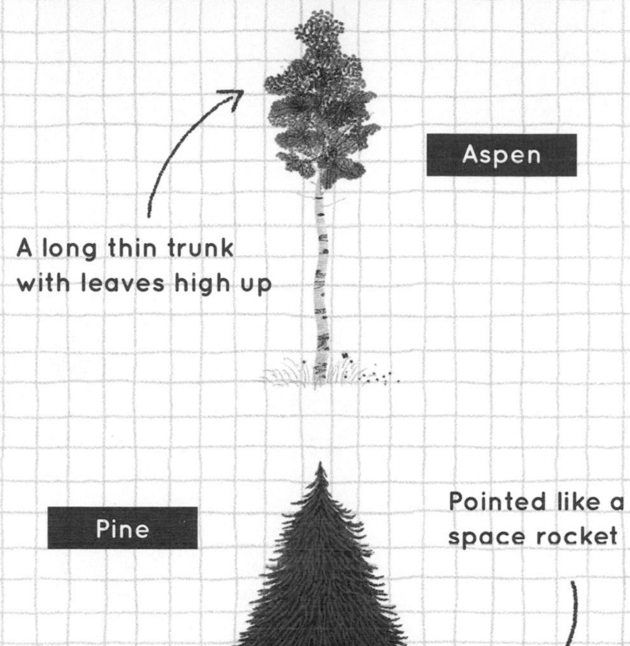

Puffy like a raincloud

Beech

A thick trunk you can stretch your arms around

Oak

Looking at the trees up close.
Which ones will we like the most?

Look what I found!

Some scratchy lumpy bark to
make a rubbing on.

Can you also see . . . ?
One twiggy bird's nest
Two squirrels racing
Three busy bumblebees

Bark is similar to our own skin because it protects the inside of the tree, keeping it safe from hot sun or icy wind.

Bark also protects trees from harmful insects. Some trees even make sticky resin that seeps out of bark like dollops of glue. It is full of chemicals that help to keep the insects away. It could make you feel ill too, so it's best not to touch it.

Trees sometimes have holes in their bark, where a branch once grew. Animals such as squirrels and birds use the holes as cosy hiding places.

Bark can be spotty or stripy, cracked or scaly. Some bark even looks like wallpaper peeling off an old wall.

Animals like deer sometimes nibble on bark. It makes a tasty snack for them but it can damage the tree too.

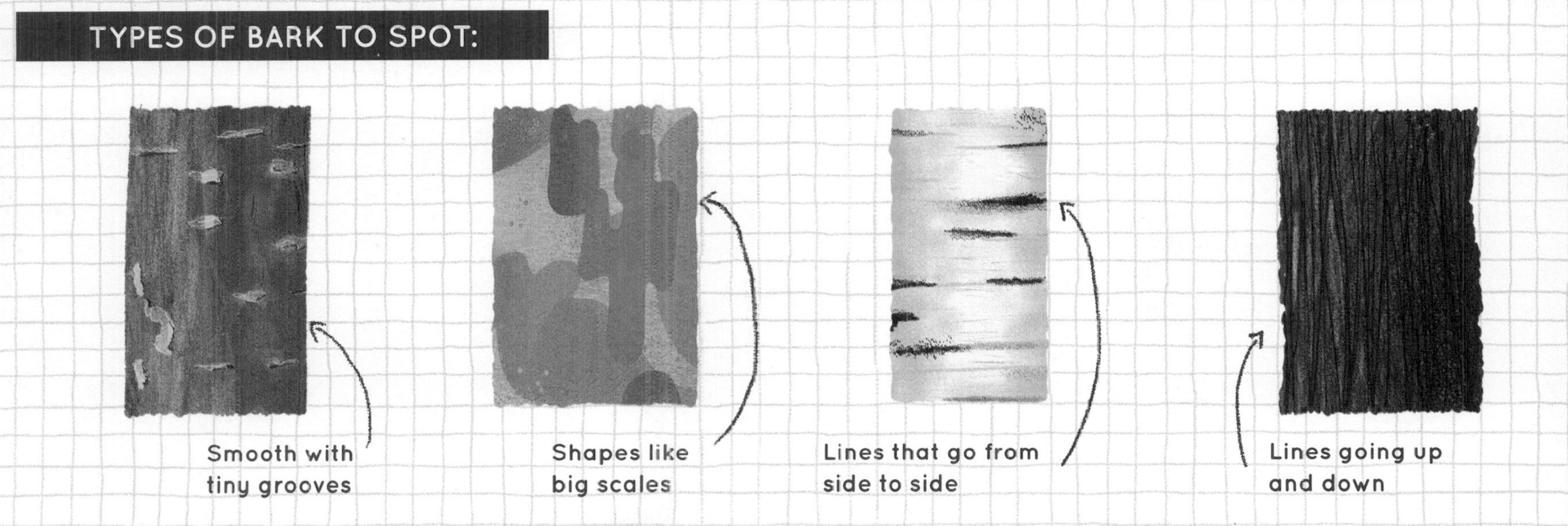

TYPES OF BARK TO SPOT:

Smooth with tiny grooves

Shapes like big scales

Lines that go from side to side

Lines going up and down

Finding treasure from the trees,
blown down by the rustling breeze.

Look what I found!

Two leaves that make funny bunny ears.

Can you also see . . . ?
One robin hopping
Two lacy spider webs
Three little purple flowers

Leaves are one of the most important parts of a tree. They use the sunlight to make a sugary food that helps the tree to grow.

If you hold a thin leaf up to the light you might be able to see lots of tiny tunnels inside it. They carry water to the leaf and they take the food that the leaf makes back to the tree.

Some trees have needles for leaves. The needles stay on their branches all year round and these trees are called 'evergreen'.

LEAF SHAPES TO SPOT:

A leaf that has wavy edges like a wiggly worm

Oak

A leaf that has jagged edges like the teeth of a zip

Birch

Maple (skeleton)

A leaf that has lost its covering, so it looks as if it is made of lace

Some trees lose their leaves in autumn. The leaves change to red, orange, yellow or brown before they fall. Trees grow new green leaves in the spring.

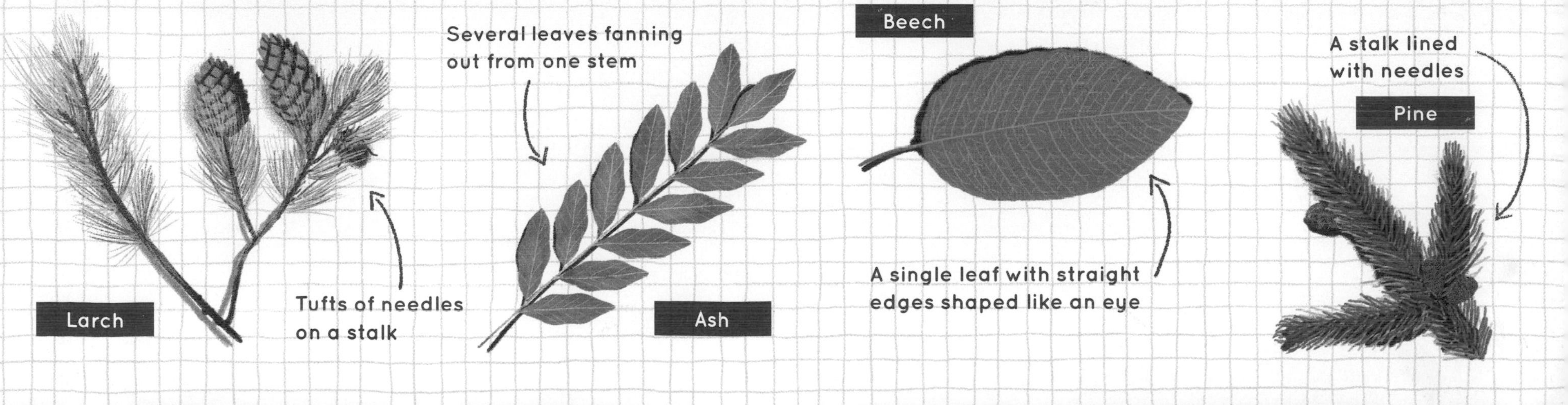

Larch

Tufts of needles on a stalk

Several leaves fanning out from one stem

Ash

Beech

A single leaf with straight edges shaped like an eye

A stalk lined with needles

Pine

Hunting underneath a tree.
What small secrets can we see?

Look what I found!

A seed like a tiny helicopter.

Can you also see . . . ?

One big blackbird

Two crawling centipedes

Three tiny wild strawberries

Some trees grow their seeds inside hard nuts. When they are ready, the nuts will fall off the tree and you can find the seeds hidden inside.

Some trees grow their seeds inside soft fruit, such as apples and pears.

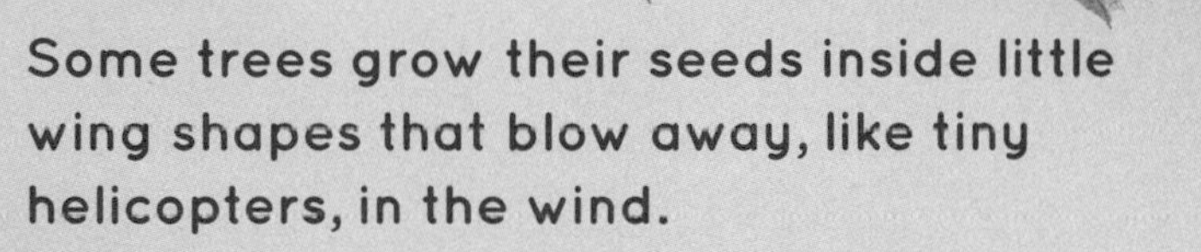

Some trees grow their seeds inside little wing shapes that blow away, like tiny helicopters, in the wind.

In the autumn, trees make seeds that fall to the ground. The seeds might one day grow into new trees.

NUTS AND NUT CASES TO SPOT:

A nut case with sharp spines

Sweet chestnut

A shiny dark nut case

Hazelnut

A spiky nut case with seeds inside

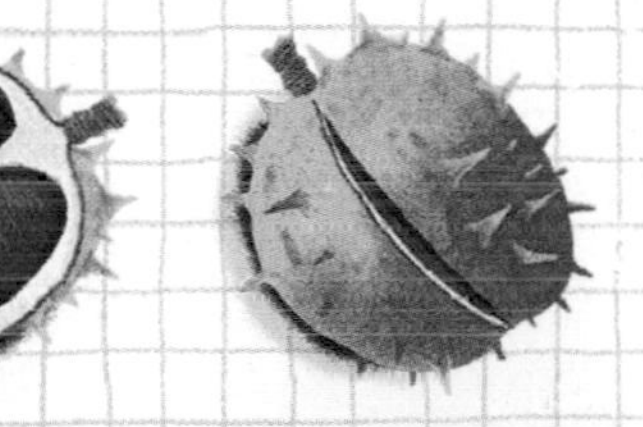

Horse chestnut

A small nut case, open like a star

Beech nut

A small nut in a cup that might have a hole in it where an animal has chewed it

Acorn

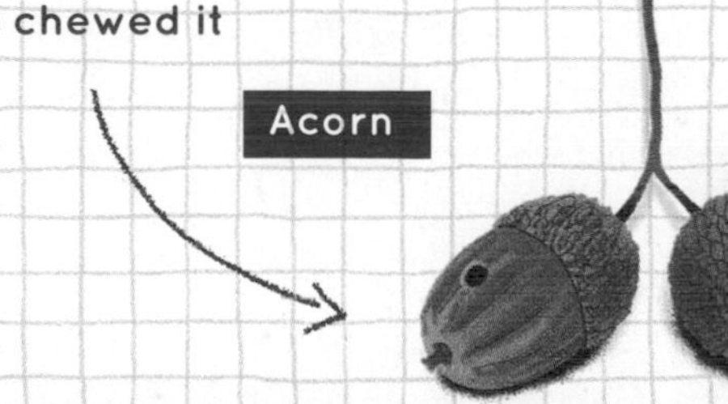

Searching in the woodland shade,
finding things the trees have made.

Look what I found!

A pine cone with its scales
stretched open like petals.

Can you also see . . . ?
One bird box where birds can nest
Two black crows
Three pink flowers

Trees that have needles grow hard cones to protect their seeds. The seeds are tucked safely under the scales of the cone, instead of inside nuts or soft fruit.

The cone scales shut tightly to protect the seeds when the weather is cold or damp.

The smallest cones are no bigger than your thumb, but the biggest ones can be as big as rugby balls.

When the weather gets warm and dry, the cone scales open and the seeds fall out, ready to grow into new trees.

CONE SHAPES TO SPOT:

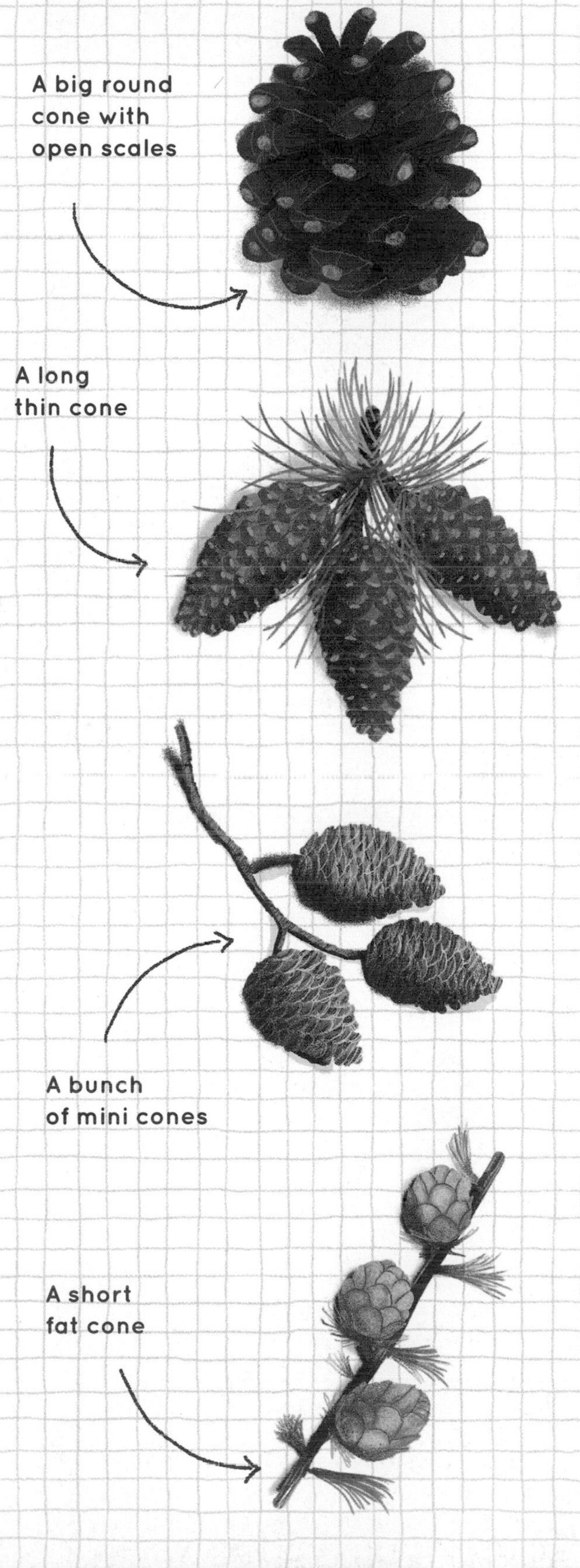

A big round cone with open scales

A long thin cone

A bunch of mini cones

A short fat cone

Spotting logs with holes inside,
where little creatures like to hide.

Look what I found!

A stripy, swirly snail shell.

Can you also see . . . ?

One slimy black slug

Two spotty ladybirds

Three shiny black beetles

A snail carries its own hiding place on its back. It can curl up and disappear inside its shell.

Be sure to only collect empty shells, so you don't harm any little snails.

Snails and slugs eat leaves and bark so the woods are a great place for them to find a meal.

Beetles might crawl inside a dead log and munch up the old wood.

Animals munch up dead wood and leaves to help keep the woods clean. They are like tiny recycling trucks, reusing the wood for their food.

Lots of woodland animals hunt other smaller creatures to eat. No wonder minibeasts like to hide!

SNAIL SHELLS TO SPOT:

A tiny shell that's round and flat

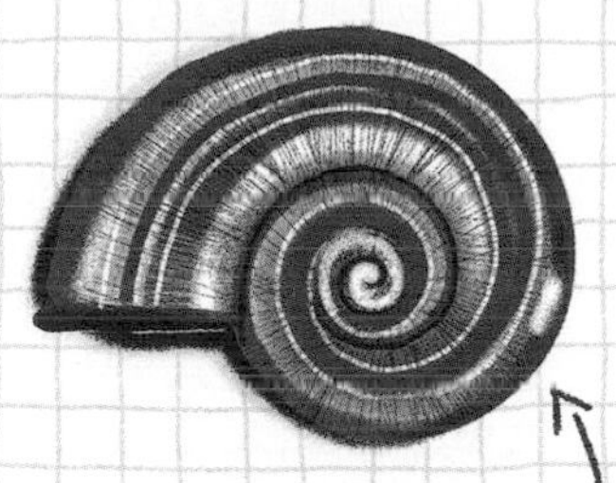

A shell with dark and light stripes

A shell that looks see-through like glass

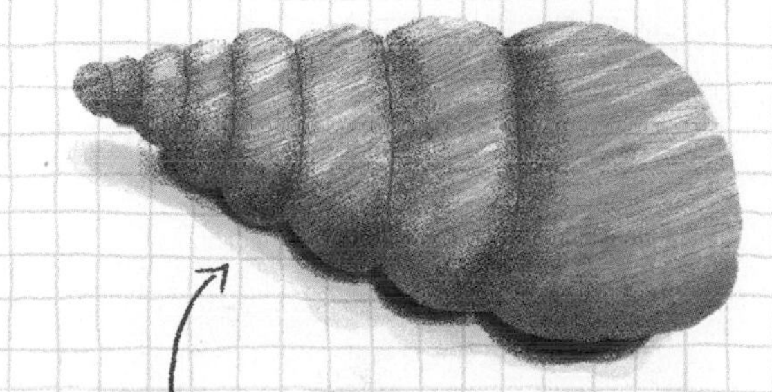

A shell that's shaped like a cone

Goodbye woods.
We're homeward bound.

Look at all the things we've found . . .

. . . TREASURE!

As you collect, be thoughtful, too.
Bring no harm with what you do.

When you're exploring the woods, only pick things up from the ground.
Never pick things from trees or flowers, or do anything that would harm animals.
That way, the woods will stay beautiful and healthy for your next visit.